Let's spread some
Christmas cheer.
Santa and his reindeer
are almost here!

Reindeer food has been a beloved tradition in our family since our girls were little. The making of reindeer food and the sprinkling of our creation in the yard right before bedtime on Christmas Eve will forever be some of our fondest holiday memories. I hope your family enjoys this treasured tradition as much as mine has!

Much Love,

Melanie Salas

Reindeer Food

A Christmas Eve Family Tradition

Created by Melanie Salas

Christmas Eve
is a very busy night,
🎅 delivers millions
of 🎁 all over the
🌍 by the 🌕's
bright light!

Dear Santa,
I hope you
are having a great
night. Thank you
for coming to
visit me!
♥

We know 🎅 needs to refuel and to eat.

So we always leave some yummy 🥧 treats.

But what about the 🦌🦌 ?

They are
important too!
They work so very
hard bringing
to you.

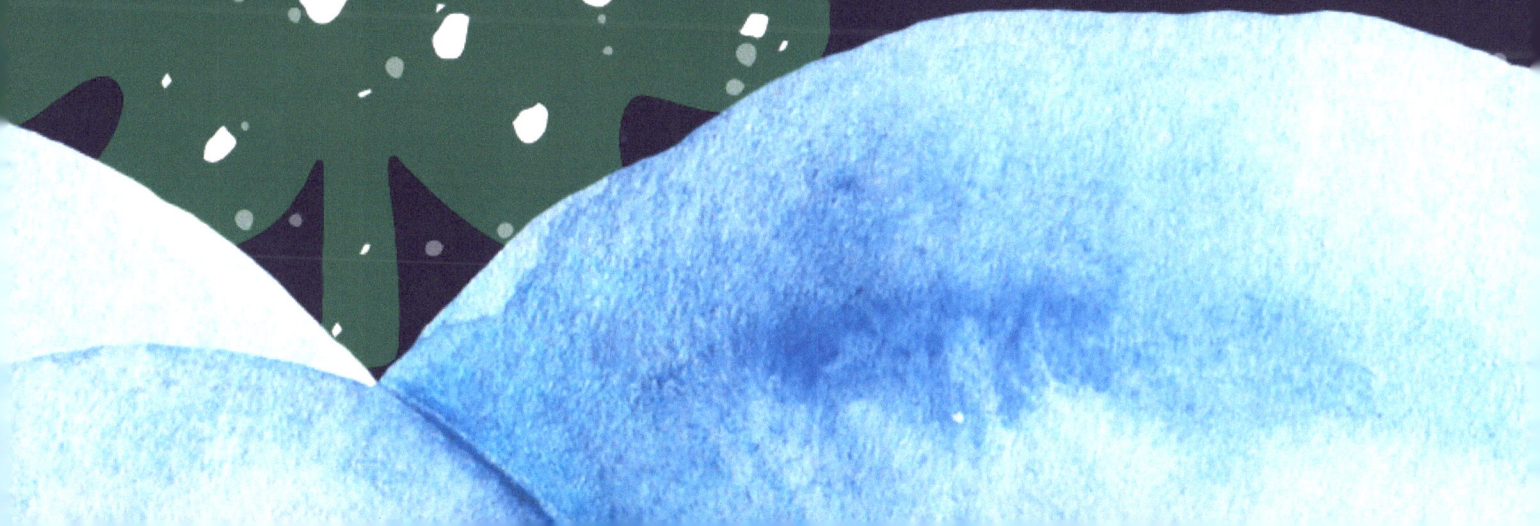

They spend all
Christmas Eve night
transporting in the sky,
and we often forget to thank
them for all the miles
that they fly.

Let's make the reindeer an extra special treat!

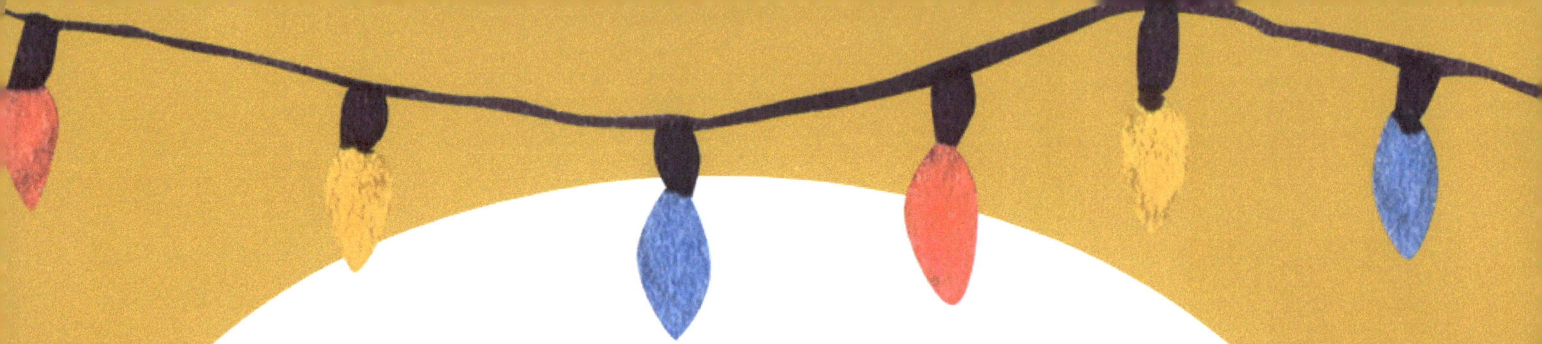

Grab some oats
and some glitter crystals
that glow!

Mix and Stir

until it's just right!
Then sprinkle in your yard
on Christmas Eve night.

The sparkle will be seen
high up in the sky,

Ensuring the
don't miss your house
and fly on by.

They will love the special treat
while 🎅 is arranging your 🎁
under your 🎄 perfectly and neat.

Once the 🦌🦌 tummies are full,
they will be ready for 🎅
to jump back in the
sleigh for them to pull.

And you will hear 🎅 exclaim
as they fly out of sight,

**"Merry Christmas to all,
and to all a good night!"**

TOP SECRET

Reindeer Food Recipe

Ingredients:

- 1 cup uncooked oats
- colored sugar crystals

1. Gather all your ingredients.
2. In a medium bowl, stir in the oats.
3. Add just the right amount of sugar crystals until your Reindeer Food sparkles and shines.
4. On Christmas Eve, just before bed, sprinkle the Reindeer Food in your yard.
5. Now, head to bed—Santa is on his way!

Reindeer Food
Published by Golden Crown Publishing, LLC

www.PolkaDotZebraPublishing.com

© 2021 Golden Crown Publishing, LLC

Created by Melanie Salas
ISBN: 978-1-954648-70-8

www.ingramcontent.com/pod-product-compliance
Lightning Source LLC
LaVergne TN
LVHW072101070426
835508LV00002B/220